LATER ELEMENTARY TO EARLY INTERMEDIATE

WEIGHTLESS

BY JASON SIFFORD

ISBN 978-1-5400-8155-1

WILLIS MUSIC

EXCLUSIVELY DISTRIBUTED BY

HAL•LEONARD®

Visit Hal Leonard Online at
www.halleonard.com

Contact us:
Hal Leonard
7777 West Bluemound Road
Milwaukee, WI 53213
Email: info@halleonard.com

In Europe, contact:
Hal Leonard Europe Limited
42 Wigmore Street
Marylebone, London, W1U 2RN
Email: info@halleonardeurope.com

In Australia, contact:
Hal Leonard Australia Pty. Ltd.
4 Lentara Court
Cheltenham, Victoria, 3192 Australia
Email: info@halleonard.com.au

FROM THE COMPOSER

The pieces in this collection were written to give teachers and students a variety of different learning experiences. "Toccata-Rocket," "Wild's Journey," and "Jupiter's Eye" are traditional recital and festival solos, guaranteed to make a lasting impression on your audience. "Enceladus" is a contemporary lyric solo that explores different meters. "Weightless," "Shining Sol," and "Dodging Asteroids" are shorter, patterned pieces that can be learned and mastered more quickly by students with limited practice time. "The Sea of Tranquility" is a predominantly black-key piece that, while sophisticated, can be taught by rote. "Lost in the Oort Cloud" is an impressionistic prelude that explores unusual harmonies and textures, while "Spacetime" investigates modern rhythmic devices like mixed meter and unusual time signatures.

PERFORMANCE NOTES

TOCCATA-ROCKET

We begin with a piece that tests our abilities at the keyboard. Launch into the first theme with precision and power, and keep the intensity up through the quiet middle section as we break orbit and begin our exploration of the solar system.

WEIGHTLESS

Feel your arms floating just above the keyboard and approach this piece with a light touch. Note the open pedal at the beginning and end—most teachers will tell you not to pedal your scales, but here in zero gravity, all the rules are a little bit different!

SHINING SOL

The word "Sol" has two meanings here. It is the name of our sun (and why we call it the "solar" system.) In music, it can also be the name of the note G, which appears shining at the top of the staff as the harmonies shift underneath.

WILD'S JOURNEY

In 1973, American astronomer Elizabeth Roemer observed a comet that had been predicted to reappear by Swiss astronomer Paul Wild. The comet, named 63P/Wild, then disappeared, only to reappear in 1999 and again in 2013. Will it be back in 2026? And what will it have encountered on its speedy journey through our solar system?

THE SEA OF TRANQUILITY

This lunar landmark is the site where the first humans landed on the moon. Imagine your right wrist jumping in a low-gravity environment as it navigates the black keys up and down the keyboard.

DODGING ASTEROIDS

Think fast! This piece is deceptively tricky; one moment you're playing slurs, the next, you're playing staccato, then slurs, then staccato. Mind your articulation carefully, and at the caesura (also called "railroad tracks"), stop and look both ways before you finally escape the asteroid belt!

ENCELADUS (pronounced "en–SEL–ə–dəs")

The rise and fall of the musical lines reflect the strange currents of the underground oceans on this mysterious moon of Saturn. Occasionally, the water and ice from these oceans erupt into space, becoming a part of the planet's famous rings.

SPACETIME

The famous physicist Albert Einstein discovered that time can change. All you have to do is travel at the speed of light. Here on Earth, we can't change time, but we can certainly change time signatures! Count carefully though—5/8 time, like quantum physics, is weird.

LOST IN THE OORT CLOUD

This region of space is so far away that it is almost a complete mystery. Too difficult to see clearly with any telescope, all we get is an impression of what it might be like. This piece is impressionistic in character, full of unusual sounds and strange harmonies. Explore them like you would the farthest reaches of our solar system, with great imagination and a sense of wonder.

JUPITER'S EYE

This "Great Red Spot" on Jupiter is actually a giant storm—larger than the planet Earth and active for more than 200 years. Capture the feeling of swirling winds in your wrists as you play. The left wrist always moves clockwise, and the right wrist moves counter-clockwise.

CONTENTS

Toccata-Rocket

Jason Sifford

Fast ♩ = 168

* Top notes of all arpeggios can be played by crossing the L.H. over

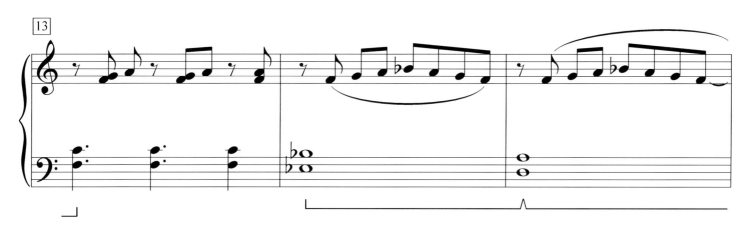

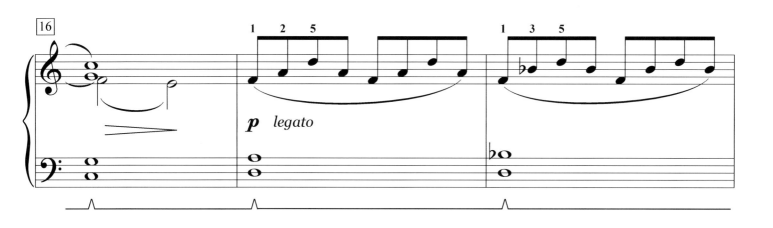

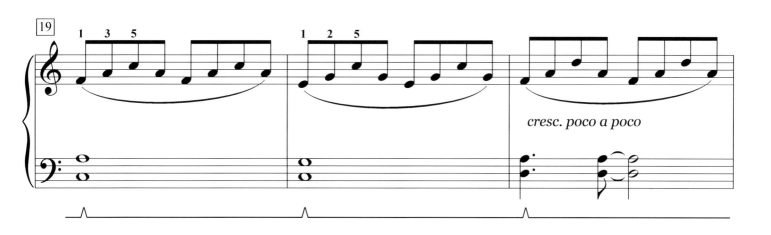

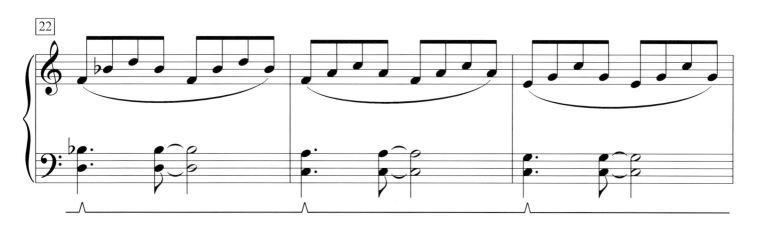

5

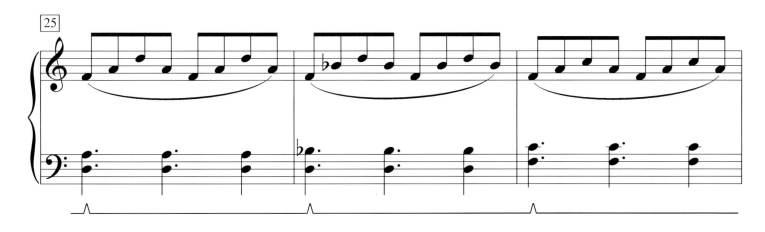

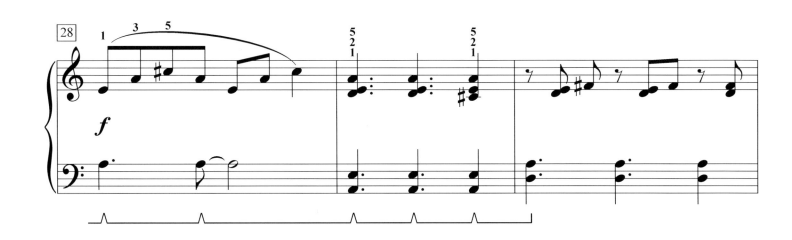

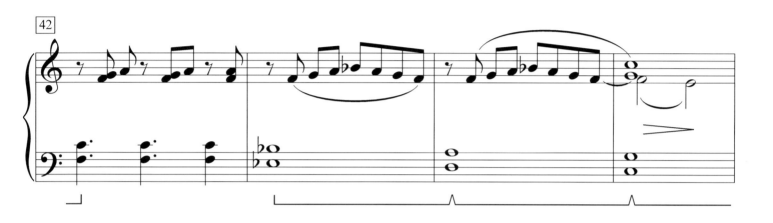

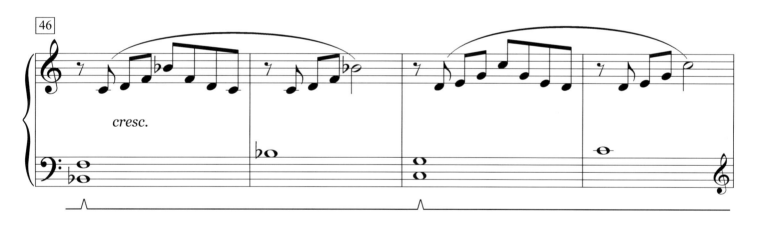

Weightless

Jason Sifford

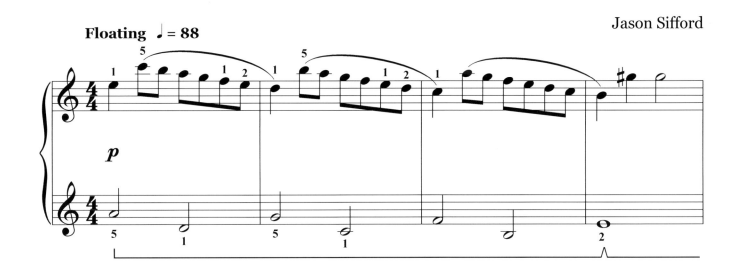

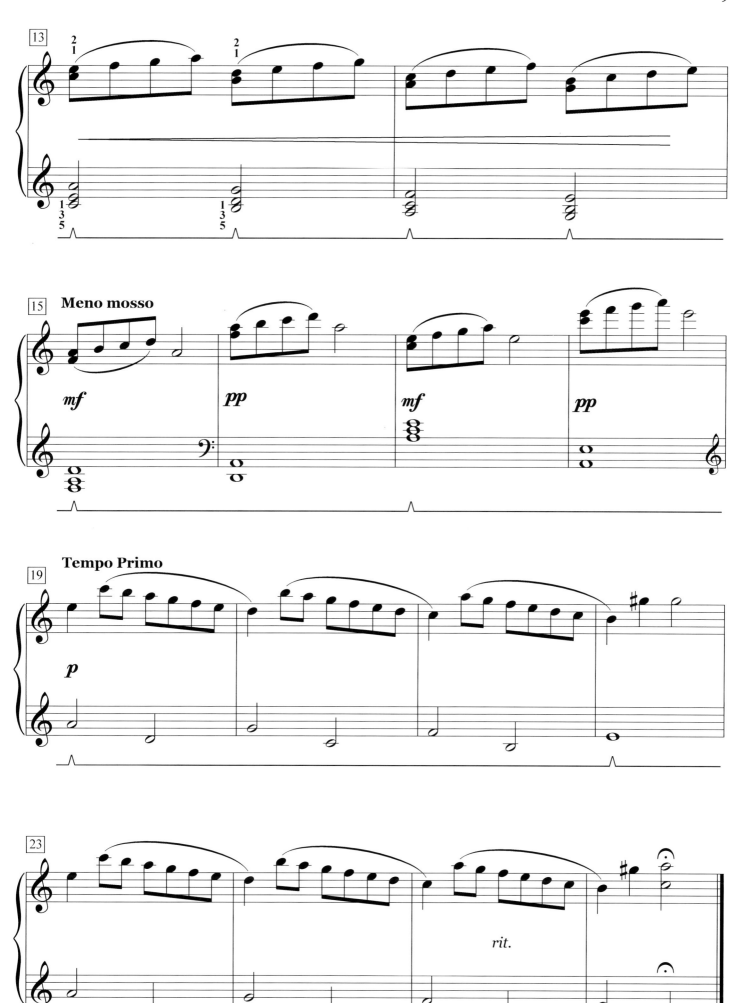

Shining Sol

for Nelda

Jason Sifford

Wild's Journey

Jason Sifford

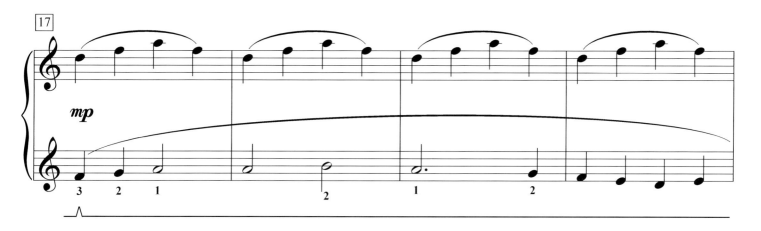

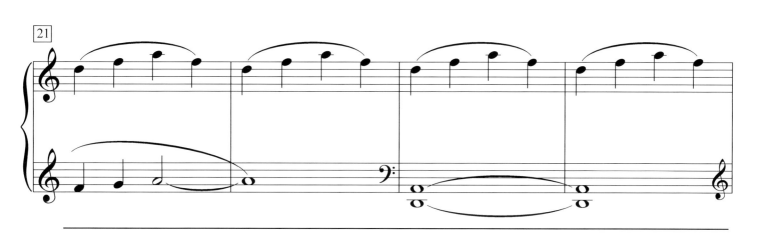

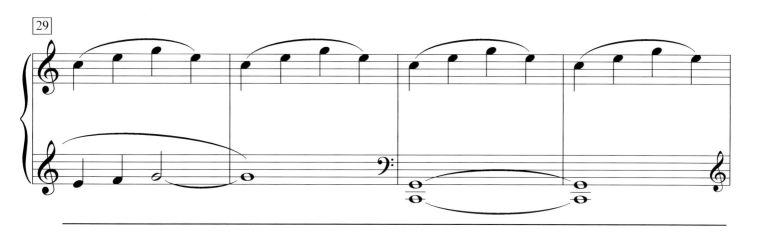

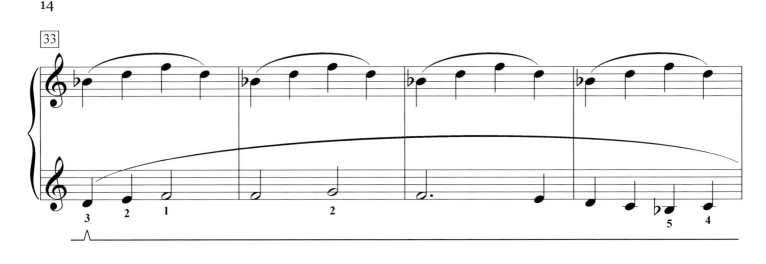

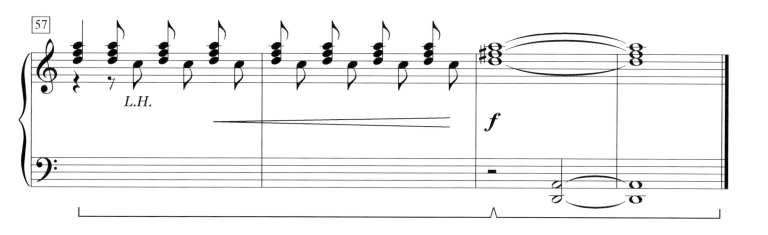

The Sea of Tranquility

Jason Sifford

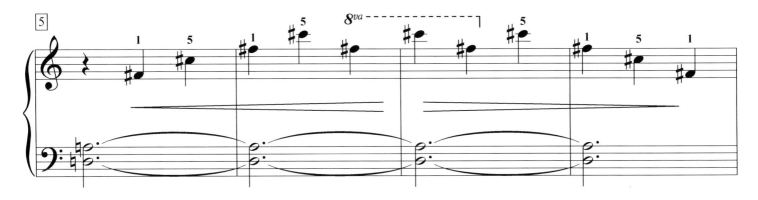

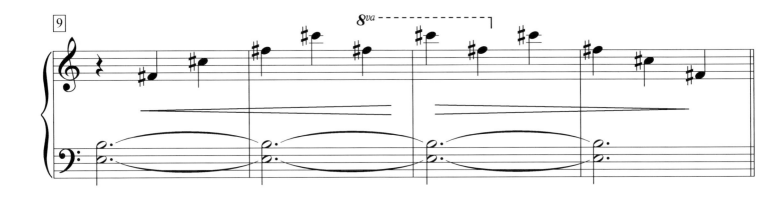

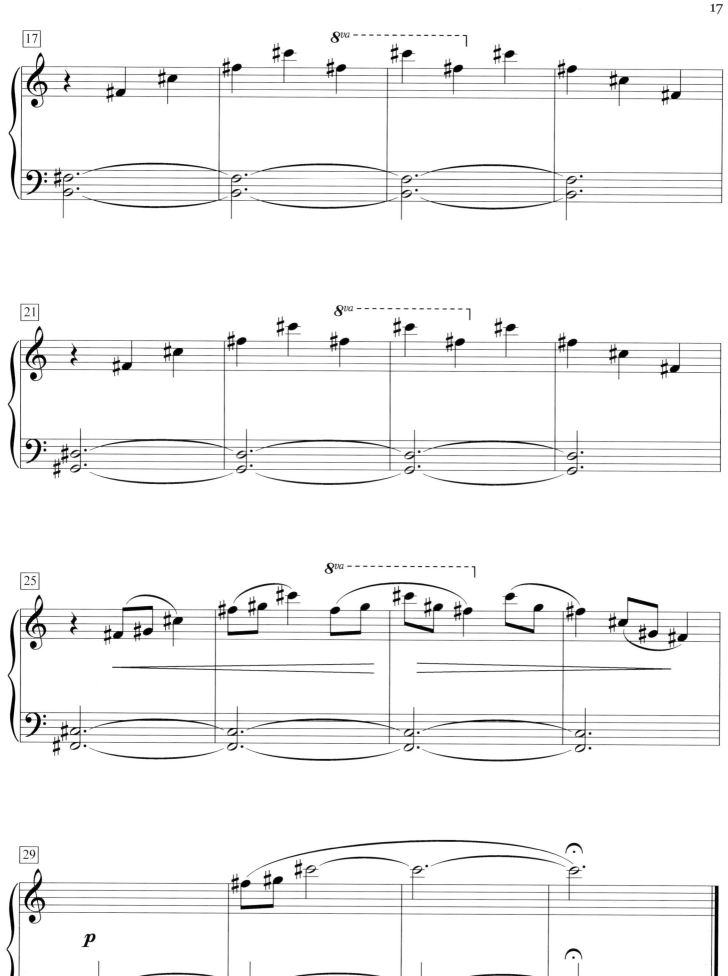

Dodging Asteroids

Jason Sifford

Enceladus

Jason Sifford

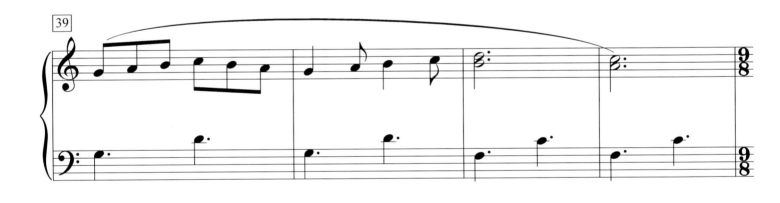

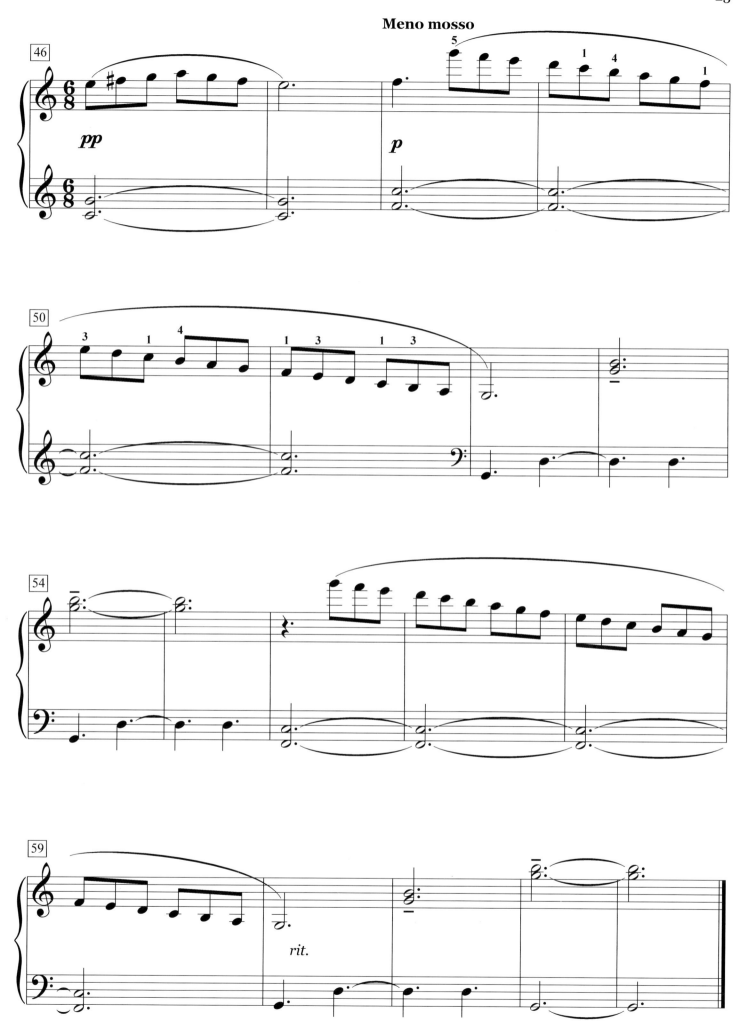

Spacetime

Jason Sifford

Lost in the Oort Cloud

Jason Sifford

keep pedal down through m.12

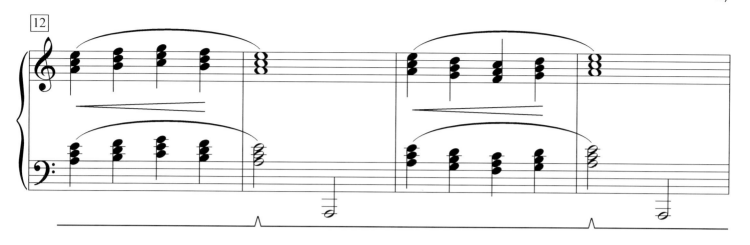

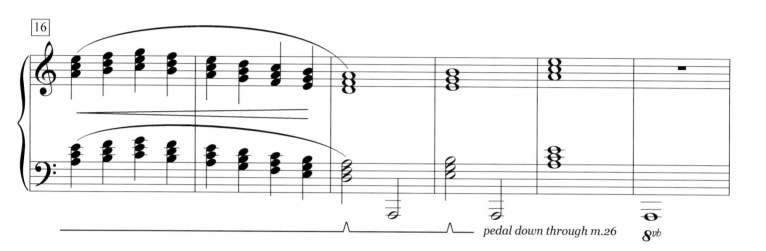

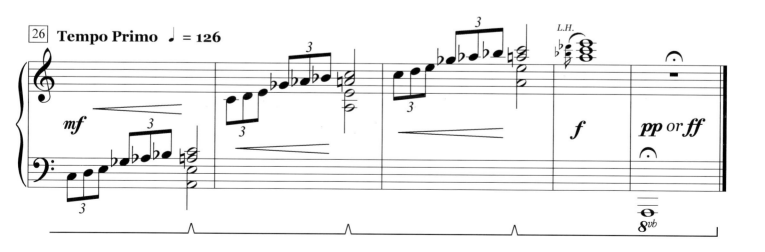

Jupiter's Eye

For the students of Linda Kennedy in Maumelle, Arkansas

Jason Sifford

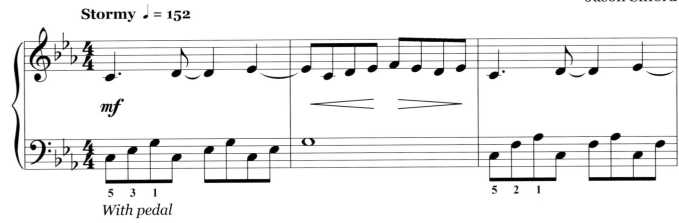

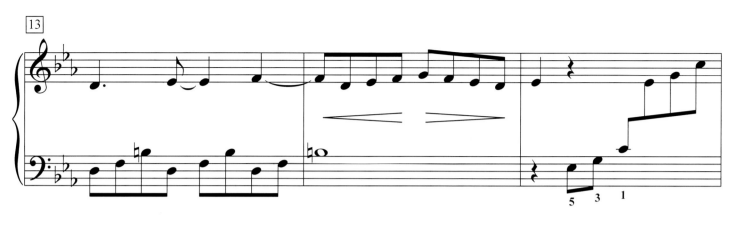

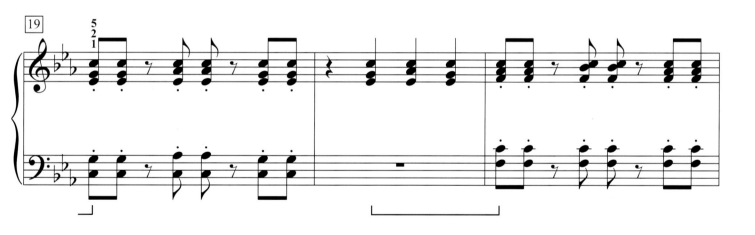

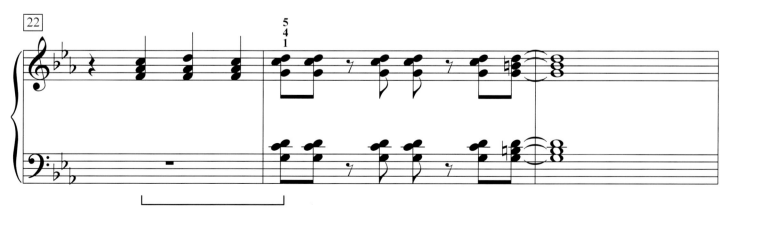

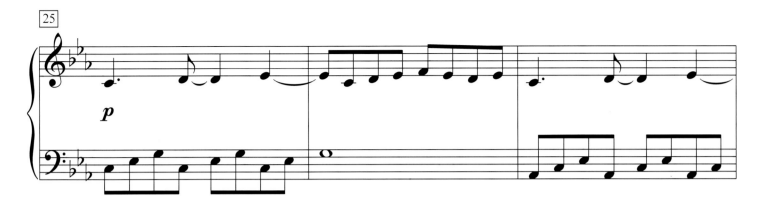

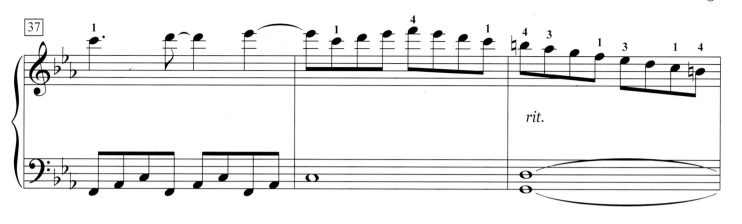

ABOUT THE COMPOSER

DR. JASON SIFFORD is a freelance pianist, teacher, and composer. He teaches at Cornell College (Iowa), maintains a private teaching studio in Iowa City, and is in demand as an adjudicator and clinician, lecturing on such diverse topics as classical performance practice, jazz pedagogy, technical development in young pianists, composition, and music technology. He also appears regularly as a music director and theater musician.

As a composer, Dr. Sifford is primarily interested in didactic literature for the piano, and his catalogue includes several solo collections, a baroque suite, and arrangements of popular and traditional songs. His music is featured in the state syllabi for Iowa and Minnesota, the bulletin for the National Federation of Music Clubs, and the Royal Conservatory of Music (Canada). Dr. Sifford holds degrees from Missouri State University, Louisiana State University, and The University of Michigan.

For more information, visit **www.jasonsifford.com.**

ALSO BY JASON SIFFORD

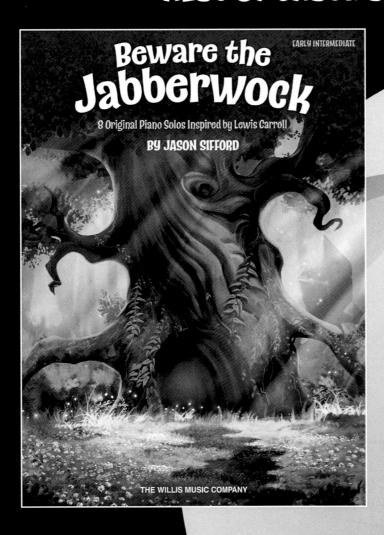

**8 Original Solos
Inspired by Lewis Carroll**
Beware the Jabberwock
Galumphing
In the Wabe
O Frabjous Day!
Snicker-Snack
The Tum-tum Tree
'Twas Brillig
Whiffling Through the Tulgey Wood

HL00290023